The Acid Test for Biblical Salvation

Dr. J.I. Parker

ISBN:

PREFACE

We were made to live forever. Our first parents were made in the **Image of God**, which is Love (Genesis 1:26,27; 1 John 5:8,16). They were blessed to **Increase His Glory** by bringing forth, through pro-creation, Life and to have dominion [rule] over every living thing moving on the earth (Genesis 1:28). In their perfect state they were called "*very good*", which means they were the **Influence of Goodness**, or as Jesus says, "*the Light of the world*"
(Genesis 1:31; Matthew 5:14). The first male and female were called "*Adam, in the day they were created*" (Genesis 5:2).

The Fall (Genesis 3)

An angel named "Lucifer", which means light bearer1[1], was created for the purpose "to minister for them who shall be heirs of salvation" (Hebrew 1:14). Prefect in his ways from "the day" he was created, but not wanting to serve, which is the greatest position in heaven like Jesus Christ [Mark 10:43-44], Lucifer, choosing not to fear the LORD, used his own corrupted wisdom to implant thoughts and imaginations in the mind of Eve. His expressed words toward Eve implied that God did not love them in commanding them not to eat of this one tree of "the knowledge of good and evil". He failed to mention the fact that they could eat of all the other trees "freely" (Genesis 2:16,17). He also said that their life would not leave them, and their light of wisdom would be greater, which was far from the Truth. He led them to imagine they would become a God, which was a lie, and so they ate the forbidden fruit. Eve was deceived, but Adam rebelled; Adam saw God create the Garden of Eden (Genesis 2:7,8; I Timothy 2:12,13). Right away their loyal love for God was gone,

---

[1] 3,458 BIBLE PEOPLE & PLACES, Copyright © 1995 by Thomas Nelson, Inc. First Inspirational Press edition published in 2001, pp.219

they failed to faithfully believe God's Word. Right away their light from within went out and they saw themselves as naked. Right away they were dying in sin and continued to die until they were dead, which is the meaning of the phrase *"thou shalt surely die"* (Genesis 2:17).

This test of God revealed the heart of Lucifer who became the tempter and when his temptation ran its course it brought forth death to our first parents (James 1:14,15). God never tempts, but he will place a test before us to choose to believe the testimony of the Word of God and with loyalty love God (James 1:15). James says:

> *"Blessed is the man that endureth temptation: for when he is tried, he shall receive the crown of life, which the Lord hath promised to them that love him."*
>
> James 1:12

The question we are forced to answer is: Do I love God with all my heart? If the freewill choice is yes, then we believe the testimony of His Word which says:

> *"For God so **loved** the world, that he gave his only begotten Son, that whosoever believeth in him should not perish, but have everlasting **life**."*
>
> John 3:16

> *"And this is the condemnation, that **light** is come into the world, and men loved darkness rather than **light**, because their deeds were evil."*
>
> John 3:19

Notice the word *"light"* is mentioned twice in this one verse. Twice mentioned in Scripture establishes a matter is of God (Genesis 41:32; Deuteronomy 19:15). Jesus gave

His life, which is the Love of God manifested to us by the Holy Spirit as the Light of the world, for the express purpose of giving whosoever that will receive Him Life.

After the prophecy and the promise made by the LORD God, which was the *alpha* sacrifice that pointed to the *omega* sacrifice of Jesus Christ [Genesis 3:15,20; Revelation 1:8], Adam named his wife *"Eve"*, which means *mother of all living* or *life giving*[2] (Genesis 3:20). Naming his wife "Eve" was his statement of faith in the promise *"the seed of the woman"* [Genesis 3:15] to come which would crush the serpent's head. That "Seed" is the prophecy of the virgin born Son of God, for a woman does not have a seed (Galatians 3:16). Deliverance from sin has always been by grace through faith (Ephesians 2:9-10).

A person might ask: Of all the voices in the world, what is truth? How do we know the difference between false religion and true religion? Of all the spiritual voices in the world, who should we listen to? Can a person know they are eternally secured? What light can be given to us that we might know that we are truly saved?

This study of the First Epistle of John is for the express purpose of identifying those truths John has set forth for us that proves a person is a true believer.

"Examine yourselves, whether ye be in the faith; prove your own selves, how that Jesus Christ is in you, except ye be reprobates?"

2 Corinthians 13:5

---

[2] 3,458 BIBLE PEOPLE & PLACES, Copyright © 1995 by Thomas Nelson, Inc. First Inspirational Press edition published in 2001, pp.111

This book is dedicated to the express purpose of helping people know they are truly saved. It is my hope that you [the reader] will not only enjoy this study, but that you will know personally - by the Word of God through the questions put forth - that you are Saved! May the love of God, the life of Christ and the light of the Holy Spirit you have received urge you to pass it on!

> *"The grace of the Lord Jesus Christ, and the love of God, and the communion of the Holy Ghost, be with you. Amen."*
>
> 2 Corinthians 13:14

Dr. Jeff I. Parker Th.D.

Eternity is too long to get it wrong.

"Wherefore the rather, brethren, give diligence to make your calling and election sure: for if ye do these things, ye shall never fall."
2 Peter 1:10

"Examine yourselves, whether ye be in the faith; prove your own selves. Know ye not your own selves, how that Jesus Christ is in you, except ye be reprobates?"
2 Corinthians 13:5

DEDICATION

I wish to dedicate this book to my wife, Priscilla, who has supported me in the publication of this book.

To my children Jeffery, Julie, John [Alex], and Alexia, for the furtherance of their Biblical Education.

To Daniel Godfrey, Associational Director of Broad River for his passion to reach the lost through the churches of Cherokee County and surrounding areas.

To my Pastor friends, Dr. Keith Harrill, Rev. Jimmy Clark, and Rev. Justin Garret who were great encouragers of this project.

To Pam Clark, whose teaching skills were helpful in proofreading the manuscript that assisted in preparing it for publication.

To Allen L. Elder who help rearrange the contents of the book for publication.

ULTIMITELY, to our ***LORD***, and ***Savior Jesus Christ!***

CONTENTS

FOREWORD

ALLEN L. ELDER

Each person who has believed on the Lord Jesus Christ in his or her heart and who have confessed Him with his or her mouth has eternal salvation. This is a Biblical reality. Unfortunately, not all these believers have a personal assurance of this salvation. In his short, little letter, the Apostle John included more than sixty references to the evidence of eternal salvation. And in this book, Dr. Parker has shown us the evidence that we may know that we are saved.

I can think of two great uses for this book. One, a pastor or teacher could preach or teach this vital information from First John directly from these anointed, accurate, alliterated, expository outlines. And two, the person who is unsure of his or her salvation could take this book along with the Bible and find the assurance of salvation that is there to be had.

With every confidence, I commend this work to you with a prayer that God will use it to settle this issue of the assurance of salvation in your heart.

For His Purpose and Glory,
Rev. Allen L. Elder
The Life Network

INTRODUCTION

This first epistle of John is the book I use with new believers to establish them in the faith. I tell them to read a chapter a day and after the fifth day start over again until they have read the epistle seven times.

They are also given these five key words to meditate on.

Chapter One – Sin
Chapter Two – Scripture
Chapter Three – Sonship
Chapter Four – Spirits
Chapter Five – Surety

Highlight the multiple times the words:
Life – Light –Love appears in the text.

Afresh and anew, receive the love of God. Be renewed in the life of Christ. Reflect the light of the Holy Spirit to your neighbors.

Until He Comes!!!

Dr. J. I. Parker

THAT YOU MAY KNOW

Expository Outlines

John's First Epistle

Am I Sensitive to Sin?

(1 John 1:8)

There are seven implications within this chapter that are there to help the believer to be sensitive to sin. The first is seen in the:

I. Foundation in Jesus (1 John 1:1)

"the Word of life"

The phrase *"from the beginning"* is found nine times in First John; twice in third John and the Gospel of John begins with the words *"In the beginning"* (John 1:1).

II. Faith in Jesus (1 John 1:2)

"eternal life"

III. Fellowship with Jesus (1 John 1:3)

"fellowship with us"

(A) Is fellowship with God (v.3b)

(B) Is fellowship with other Believers (v.3a)

IV. Fullness in Jesus (1 John 1:4)

The revealed Word of Life from the beginning is for the expressed purpose of: Receiving – Restoring – Reverberating the fellowship with God available to whosoever through God.

V. Following Jesus (1 John 1:5)

"God is light, and in him is no darkness at all"

(A) God is Life (John 1:1-3; John 14:6; 1 John 1:1)

God the Son

(B) God is Light (1 John 1:5)

God the Holy Spirit

(C) God is Love (1 John 4:8, 16)

God the Father

VI. Forsaking Jesus (1 John 6, 8, 10)

(A) There is No Light (v.6)

(B) There is No Love (v.8)

(C) There is No Life (v.10)

VII. Forgiveness in Jesus (1 John 1:7; 9)

(A) Is a Choice in our Walk (v.7)

(B) Is a Confess in our Word (v.9)

Conclusion: True believers who do not doubt they are saved, *walk in the light*, *work in the life* and *witness to others the love of God!*

Am I Submissive to Scripture?

(1 John 2:1-29)

Speaking to believers, John says true believers will continue to reveal their standing with all believers.

I. Scripture Gives Light on Who We Should Love (1 John 2:1-14)

(A) An expression of Love (2:1-6)

(B) An Expression of Light (2:7-14)

II. Scripture Gives Light on What We Should Not Love (1 John 2:15-17)

(A) The Warning of Scripture (v.15)

(B) The Way of the Serpent (v.16)

(C) The Way of Sin (v.17a)

(D) The Way of the Savior (v.17b)

III. Scripture Gives Light on How Love is Revealed as Life (1 John 2:18-29)

(A) End-time People who live the life of the Lie

(2:18-26)

(1) They are many in the world (v.18)

(2) They will not continue with us (v.19)

(3) They don't have an Unction from the Holy One (v.20)

(4) They know not the Truth (1:6)

(5) They are liars who consistently deny Christ (v.22, 23)

(6) They are seducers (v.26)

(B) Eternal People who live the Life of the Truth (2:20-25)

(1) They have an Unction from the Holy One (v.20)

(a) Unction is Light (1:5)

(b) Unction is Love (2:5)

(c) Unction is Life (2:25)

(2) They have Overcome the Wicked One (2:14-16)

(3) They have Fellowship with God (1:7a)

(4) They continue with Other Believers (1:7b)

(5) They Live the Truth They Know Consistently (2:22-25)

Conclusion: Believers view Scripture as the Truth from the beginning.

Am I Submerged into Sonship?

(1 John 3:1-24)

Here are four human facets revealed in those who are submerged into Sonship. First, there is:

I. A Conviction of Sonship (1 John 3:1-6)

(A) Description of His People (vs.1-3)

(1) Love – Directly made to be (v.1)

(2) Hope – Determined to be (v.2)

(3) Faith – Declared to be (v.4)

(B) Direction of His Purity (vs.4-6)

II. A Consciousness of Sonship (1 John 3:7-14)

(A) Actions (vs.7,8)

(1) Followers of the Savior (v.7, 9)

(2) Followers of Satan (v.8)

(B) Attitudes (vs.9-11)

(1) Note the hatred of Cain

(2) Note the love of Abel

(C) Answers (vs.12-14)

(1) Cain's is evil

(2) Abel's is righteous

III. A Confidence Of Sonship (1 John 3:15-22)

(A) A Compassion in the heart (vs.15-18)

(B) A Comparison of the heart (v.19)

(C) A Condemned heart (vs.20-22)

IV. A Commandment of Sonship (1 John 3:22-24)

Conclusion: True believers have all four human facets that John has shared in this chapter, which submerges them into Sonship.

Am I Sharing the Truth in the Spirit?

(1 John 4:1-21)

The first time we see the phrase *"Hereby know ye"* relates to the:

I. Fact of the Spirits (1 John 4:1-6a)

(A) The Spirt of Christ (vs.2,4,6a)

(B) The Spirit of Antichrist (vs.3,5,6b)

II. Fruit of the Spirit (1 John 4:6b-10)

(A) Love is an expression of God (v.7)

(B) Love is the essence of God (v.8)

(1) To Reveal the Savior (v.9a)

(2) To Reclaim the Sinner (v.9b)

(3) To Reflect through the Saints (v.10)

III. Followers of the Sprit (1 John 4:11-16)

(A) They Perform in the Love of God (v,11)

(B) They are Perfected in the Love of God (v.12)

(C) They are Presently in the Love of God (vs.13-16)

(1) We now have the Spirit of God (v.13,14)

God is Light

(2) We now are in the Son of God (v.15)

God the Life

(3) We now are in God the Father (v.16)

God is Love

IV. Formation of the Spirit (1 John 4:17-21)

(A) Scripture develops our Faith

(B) Sharing our Faith

(C) Situations of Faith

Conclusion: All true believers are indwelled with the Spirit of God (Romans 8:9). True Spirit-filled people will consistently confess that Christ has come in the flesh.

Am I Sharing the Truth in the Spirit?

(1 John 4:1-21)

The first time we see the phrase *"Hereby know ye"* relates to the:

I. Fact of the Spirits (1 John 4:1-6a)

(A) The Spirt of Christ (vs.2,4,6a)

(B) The Spirit of Antichrist (vs.3,5,6b)

II. Fruit of the Spirit (1 John 4:6b-10)

(A) Love is an expression of God (v.7)

(B) Love is the essence of God (v.8)

(4) To Reveal the Savior (v.9a)

(5) To Reclaim the Sinner (v.9b)

(6) To Reflect through the Saints (v.10)

III. Followers of the Sprit (1 John 4:11-16)

(A) They Perform in the Love of God (v,11)

(B) They are Perfected in the Love of God (v.12)

(C) They are Presently in the Love of God (vs.13-16)

(4) We now have the Spirit of God (v.13,14)

God is Light

(5) We now are in the Son of God (v.15)

God the Life

(6) We now are in God the Father (v.16)

God is Love

IV. Formation of the Spirit (1 John 4:17-21)

(A) Scripture develops our Faith

(B) Sharing our Faith

(C) Situations of Faith

Conclusion: All true believers are indwelled with the Spirit of God (Romans 8:9). True Spirit-filled people will consistently confess that Christ has come in the flesh.

Am I Saved for Sure?

(1 John 5:1-21)

I. Saving Faith (1 John 5:1-5)

(A) Is Ongoing Faith (vs.1-3)

(1) Has consistent Life in His Son (v.1) *"believeth"*

(2) Has consistent Light in His Spirit (v.2) *"we know"*

(3) Has consistent Love in God the Father (v.3) *"this is the love of God"*

(B) Is Overcoming Faith (vs.4,5)

II. Sovereign Facts (1 John 5:6-12)

(A) The Truth of God (v.6)

(B) The Tri-unity of God (v.7)

(1) God the Father

(2) God the Son

(3) God the Holy Ghost

(C) The Testimony of God (v.8)

(1) The Spirit

(2) The Scripture – *"the water"*

(3) The Sacrifice – *"the blood"*

(D) The Teachers of God (vs.9-12)

(1) Teach the Word of God (v.9)

(2) Believe the Record of God (v.10)

(3) Have eternal Life in God (vs.11,12)

III. Saved Forever (1 John 5:13-21)

(A) Clarity of Life (v.12)

(B) Confirmation of Life (v.13)

(C) Confidence of Life (vs.14-20)

(D) Command of Life (v.21)

Conclusion: As faithful servants and stewards of God, may we raise the children born to us or simply around us in *the fear of God, the fire of the Holy Spirit*, and *the faith of a little child that was exemplified perfectly for us in the Son of God.*

THAT YOU MAY BELIEVE

Expository Commentary

John's First Epistle

CHAPTER 1
Am I Sensitive to Sin?
1 John 1:1-10

There are seven implications within this chapter that are there to help the believer to be sensitive to sin. The first is seen in the true believers':

Foundation in Jesus

"That which was from the beginning, which we have heard, which we have seen
with our eyes, which we have looked upon,
and our hands have handled, of ***the Word of***
life*"*

1 John 1:1

The phrase *"from the beginning"* is found nine times in First John; twice in third John and the Gospel of John begins with the words *"In the beginning"* (John 1:1). The psalmist says:

"If the foundations be destroyed, what can the righteous do?" Psalm 11:3

Foundational principles are important to John. If Genesis chapters 1-11 are not real history, then our faith has no sure foundation. John identifies this present-day problem and starts his books off with a sure foundation of God's Word!

The Apostle Paul made this revealing statement:
"For other foundation can no man lay than that is laid, which is Jesus Christ." 1 Corinthians 3:11

The major emphasis in the gospel of John is on the essential *deity* of the Lord Jesus Christ: the major emphasis in this epistle is on the essential *humanity* of the Lord Jesus Christ. He was God. He was man. He was both![3] If Genesis chapters 1-11 are not real history, then our faith has no sure foundation. John identifies this present-day problem and starts his books off with a sure foundation of God's Word!

Faith in Jesus

"For the life was manifested, and we have seen it, and bear witness and shew unto you that ***eternal life****, which was with the Father, and was manifested unto us."*
1 John 1:2

The *"tree of life"* is closely connected to the *"Word of life"* as well as *"the fountain of life"*.

- Eat of the tree of life and live forever (Genesis 2:9, 16; 3:22, 24)
- Jesus said eat of me and you will have eternal life (John 6:54)
- Jesus Christ is the visible proof of *"that eternal life"* (1 John 1:2)
- Jesus Christ told the woman at the well:

[3] Philips, John, EXPORTING THE EPISTLE OF JOHN, © copyright 2003, by John Phillips. Published in 2003 by Kregel Publications, Inc. pp.24

"But whosoever drinketh of the water that I shall give him shall never thirst; but the water that I shall give him shall be in him a well of water springing up into everlasting life."
John 4:14

The Old Testament says:
"The fear of the LORD is a fountain of life, to depart from the snares of death."
Proverbs 14:27

"The Fear of the LORD" here speaks of honor and respect to Jehovah. Faith in Jesus alone is eternal life!

Fellowship with Jesus

"That which we have seen and heard declare we unto you, that ye also may have fellowship with us: and truly our fellowship is with the Father, and with his Son Jesus Christ."
1 John 1:3

- Is fellowship with God (v.3b)
  "*the Father, and with the Son*"

Jesus and the Father are one (John 14:1-11).
Jesus is God! (John 20:28).

- Is fellowship with other Believers (v.3a)
  "*fellowship with us*"

Fullness in Jesus

"*And these things write we unto you, that your joy may be full.*"
1 John 1:4

The revealed Word of Life from the beginning is for the expressed purpose of: Receiving – Restoring – Reverberating the fellowship with God available to whosoever through God.

Following Jesus

"This then is the message which we have heard of him, and declare unto you, that God is light, and in him is no darkness at all"
1 John 1:5

- God is Life (John 1:1-3; John 14:6; 1 John 1:1)

God the Son

- God is Light (1 John 1:5)

God the Holy Spirit

- God is Love (1 John 4:8, 16)

God the Father

This is the message of Jesus Christ: "in Him is no darkness at all". John has said: "We have heard", "we have seen", "we have looked", "we have handled, of the Word of life", and "we declare unto you that eternal life" (1 John 1:1,2). Darkness was created by God to contrast the LIGHT (Isaiah 45:5-7).

Forsaking Jesus

1 John 6, 8, 10

- There is No Light (v.6) "*walk in darkness*"
- There is No Love (v.8) "*the truth is not in us*"
- There is No Life (v.10) "*his word is not in us*"

Remember earlier John says that Jesus is "*the Word of life*" (1 John 1:1).

Forgiveness in Jesus
1 John 1:7;9

- Is a Choice in our Walk (v.7) "*cleanseth us from all sin*"
- Is a Confession in our Word (v.9) "*cleanse us from all unrighteousness*"

Conclusion

The devil wants to deceive humanity about the faith in God; he wants to distance humanity from the hope of fellowship with God; and he want to destroy humanity from ever following God. The devil does not want us to live free from sin! Note the conditional word "If" (1 John 1:6-10). Does sin bother you? The Apostle John has explained to his readers what it means to be sensitive to sin! Anyone who can continue to sin, and it does not bother them, is a lost person. True believers who do not doubt they are saved, **walk in the light, work in the life** *and* **witness to others the love of God!**

CHAPTER 2
Am I Submissive to Scripture?
1 John 2:1-29

Speaking to believers, John says true believers will continue to reveal their standing with all believers. What sets true believers apart from those just in the group for a while like Judas? John declares:

"But ye have an unction from the Holy One, and ye know all things."
1 John 2:20

Chapter two of First John is an exposition of how believers should view the Scriptures from "*little children*" to full maturity. You will note the phrase "*from the beginning*" five times in this one chapter: which means foundational truth is being shared that has never changed. The chapter starts with identifying how the Spirit of:

Scripture Gives Light on Who We Should Love
1 John 2:1-14

An Expression of Love
1 John 2:1-6

"*My little children*" is a formal *commencement* of dearness expressed to John's readers (1 John 2:1). Do you want to do God's will? Example: A young girl wants to marry a man who has actions that are not becoming of a Christian. Ask her the question! Do you want to do God's will?

"And hereby do we know that we know him, if we keep his commandments."
1 John 2:3

Jesus once said, "Why call ye me, Lord, Lord, and do not the things which I say?" (Luke 6:46); this is a Poignant question. A familiar complaint of those who despise Christian teaching is that "Christians" don't act like Christians! It is a sad commentary on the condition of the Lord's family when the ungodly are more aware of the expected behavior of God's people than the Christians. Of course, the issue is not unique to the New Testament times. Israel's historical saga is replete with seasons of rebellion and repentance –so much so that the psalmist prayed:

"That the generation to come…. Might set their hope in God, and not forget the works of God, but keep his commandments: and might not be as their fathers, a stubborn and rebellious generation; a generation that set not their heart aright, and whose spirit was not steadfast with God."
Psalm 78:6-8

My mother-in-law, Louise Horn, wrote in her Bibles and her children's Bibles this quote from D.L. Moody which say: "This Book will keep you from sin or sin will keep you from this Book." This is true. Scripture is given to us to keep us from sin. It expresses what to do if we have sinned and encourages those who keep it of a true relationship with God (1 John 2:1-3). The Word is our Help in Persuasion (1 John 2:1). The Word is our Holiness in Purification (1 John 2:2,3). And the Word is our Hope of Perfection (1 John 2:4-6). Believers express love to God by their obedience (Matthew 7:21)!

John moves from an expression of Love to:

An Expression of Light
1 John 2:7-14

"*Brethren*" is a form of closeness in the family of God expressed to John's readers (1 John 2:7). Believers love their neighbors! "*On these two commandments*," Loving God and loving your neighbor, "*hangs all the law and the prophets*" (Matthew 22:37-40). Loving God relates to the first four of the ten commandments. Loving your neighbor relates to the last six of the ten commands. Loving your neighbor means to love those near you as family as well as those distant from you as sinners. The words "*from the beginning*" are expressed four times in this short passage regarding light and love, which is foundational to life of a true believer. Brethren are those who walk in the light and have fellowship with God and with other believers, because "*darkness is past, and the true light now shineth*" (1 John 1:7; 2:8). Believers express light in the way they refuse to hate their neighbor! Note John's intended readers are:

- "*Little children*" (v.12) – your sins are forgiven..
- "*Fathers*" (13a) – you know Him that is from the beginning..
- "*Young men*" (v.13b) – ye have overcome the wicked one..
- "*Little children*" (v.13c) – ye have known the Father.
- "*Fathers*" (v.14a) – ye have known Him that is from the beginning [repeated]
- "*Young men*" (v.14b) – ye are strong, and the word of God abides in you, and ye have overcome the wicked one. [last phrase is repeated from verse v.13b]

The emphasis by John in his first epistle, however, is not on the reasons for willful disobedience, but on the results of willing obedience.

Five results of willing obedience

1. Walking in the "light" ensures fellowship (1 John 1:7).
2. Constant and willing obedience produces and effective prayer life (1 John 3:22).
3. A Lifestyle of obedience brings an awareness of the Holy Spirit's indwelling (1 John 3:24).
4. Loving God produces obedience, which in turn brings joy in that obedience (1 John 5:3).
5. Our deeds show whom we serve (1 John 3:7). Our righteous deeds prove whom we serve (Matthew 7:16-20).

Scripture reflects light on who we should love.

Scripture Gives Light on What We Should Not Love

1 John 2:15-17

Four things we are told of to watch for are:

- The Warning of Scripture (v.15) "*love not the world, neither the things…*"
- The Way of the Serpent (v.16) "*lust of the flesh, and the lust of the eyes, and the pride of life is not of the Father, but of the world.*" These words give us the pattern of the tempter.
- The Way of Sin (v.17a) "*the world passeth away, and the lust thereof*"
- The Way of the Savior (v.17b) "*he that doeth the will of God abideth for ever*"

Believers love not the world, neither the things of this world! Scripture gives light on who we should love. Scripture gives light on what we should not love.

Scripture Gives Light on How Love is Revealed as Life

1 John 2:18-29

There are two basic groups of people in the world: those who live a lie and those who live the Truth. In the End-time they will be separated by God: one to hell and the other to heaven; one to eternal judgment and the other to eternal joy! The first group is the:

End-time People Who Live the Life of the Lie

1 John 2:18-26

The lie is found in Genesis 3: 5, "*ye shall be as gods, knowing good and evil*". Someone has said: "A lie is a kernel of truth wrapped in a lie". God commanded Adam not to eat of the tree of good and evil, which is the true Word of God (Genesis 2:17). Yes, God knows intellectually good and evil, but experientially God does not know sin. The Bible says He knew no sin, but took upon Himself our sin, "*that we might be made the righteousness of God in him*" (2 Corinthians 5:21). Jesus took upon Himself, but He never had sin in Him. Therefore, we can say without any doubt there was no sin in Jesus Christ. God does not want a mixture of good and evil for it leads to death. God is light and there is no darkness in Him at all (1 John 1:5).

John tells us six things regarding the End-time people who embrace the lie.

(1) They are many in the world (v.18)
(2) They will not continue with us (v.19)
(3) They don't have an Unction from the Holy One (v.20)

(4) They know not the Truth (1:6) "walk in darkness" (2:21) "know not the truth"
(5) They are liars who consistently deny Christ (v.22, 23)
(6) They are seducers (v.26)

Jesus said: "The thief cometh not, but for to steal, and to kill, and to destroy" (John 10:10a). Thank God that is not all Jesus said, Scripture gives light on how love is revealed as life in the life of:

Eternal People who live the Life of the Truth

1 John 2:20-25

They have an Unction from the Holy One (v.20)

Unction is a necessity for true Gospel living, teaching, and preaching. Charles Spurgeon has said, "Let us continue instant, constant, fervent in supplication. Let your fleece be on the thrashing floor of supplication till it is wet with the dew of heaven."

Unction is the arch of the chapter that brings the scripture alive to the believer. "*All scripture is given by inspiration of God, and is profitable for doctrine, for reproof, for correction, for instruction in righteousness: that the man of God may be perfect, throughly furnished unto all good works.*" 2 Timothy 3:16, 17

Unction from the Holy One is at least three things restored to true believers, lost in the fall:

- Unction is Light (1:5) "*God is light*" (2:8, 27) "*the true light now shineth…the same anointing teacheth you all things*"
- Unction is Love (2:5) "*the love of God*" (4:8, 16) "*God is love*"

- Unction is Life (2:25) "*even eternal life*"

Jesus said:
"*I am come that they might have life, and that they may have it more abundantly*" John 10:10b

You see, the lack of loyal love to the Word of God is why our first parents lost their light and life (Genesis 3:1-7).

They have overcome the wicked one (vs.14-16)

Believing God's Word is true, they have forsaken the world systems, which is to satisfy the lust of the flesh, lust of the eyes and the pride of life (2:15, 16).

They have Fellowship with God (v.7a)

"*we walk in the light*" (2:17, 29) "doeth [consistently does] the will of God…every one that doeth [consistently does] righteousness is born of Him"

They Continue with Other Believers (v.7b)

"*Fellowship one with another*" (2:10, 19) "loveth his brother abideth in the light…continued with us"

They Live the Truth They Know Consistently (vs.22-25)

"*He that acknowledgeth the Son hath the Father also…that which ye have heard from the beginning shall remain in you, ye also shall continue in the Son, and in the Father…even eternal life.*"

Conclusion

Believers view Scripture as the Truth from the beginning. By the death, burial, and resurrection of Christ we "have overcome the wicked one", which tempted our first parent to transgress against God's Word. By faith in "the Holy One" which the Father promised us from the beginning, Jesus Christ, all believers come into the Light of eternal Truth by His Love to have fellowship with God and one another, which is eternal Life (1 John 1:7; 2:5, 25). His Word must abide in us, and we must "abide in Him". This type of fellowship with God gives confidence and we will not be ashamed before Him at His coming (1 John 2:28). If you don't have fellowship with God today let:

"The grace of the Lord Jesus Christ, and the love of God, and the communion of the Holy Ghost, be with you all. Amen."
2 Corinthians 13:14

CHAPTER 3
Am I Submerged into Sonship?
1 John 3:1-24

John has been saying true believers will know if they are saved or not by the Word of God they have chosen to follow.

John shares four human facets revealed in those who are submerged into Sonship. First, there is:

A Conviction of Sonship
1 John 3:1-6

The word "manner" in the passage is *potapos*, a Greek word primarily meaning "from what country," then "of what sort."[4] There is no country on earth characterized by such love which God embodies and displays in heaven and throughout His vast creation. The Holy Spirit in the believers sets them apart from all earthly creations. John starts by giving us a:

Description of His People
1 John 3:1-3

Things that define a true follower of Jesus Christ are love, hope, and faith. "Behold" or "check it out" as a vernacular of our day.

Love – Directly made to be – "*the sons of God*" (v.1)

"*Behold, what manner of love the Father hath bestowed upon us,*

---

[4] Vine, W.E., VINE'S EPOSITIORY DICIONARY OF NEW TESAMENT WORDS, I Vol. (London: Oliphants, 1952).

that we should be called the sons of God: therefore the world knoweth us not, because it knew him not." 1 John 3:1

This passage, if not studied properly, can be misunderstood, and become obscure to the average Bible student. Understanding the phrase "*the sons of God*" is vital in gaining the full rich interpretation. The first time we see the phrase "*the sons of God*" is a reference to angels and is always a reference to them in the Old Testament. In the Book of Job, we read.

"*Now there was a day when the sons of God came to present themselves before the LORD, and Satan came also among them.*"
Job 1:6

"*And again there was a day when the sons of God came to present themselves before the LORD, and Satan came also among them to present himself before the LORD.*"
Job 2:1

The only other reference to "the son of God" that refers not to angels is found in Luke chapter three, where we have the genealogy of Adam.

"*Which was the son of Enos, which was the son of Seth, which was the son of Adam, which was the son of God.*"
Luke 3:38

Why would Adam be called "*the son of God*"? Adam, like angels were direct creations of God. All of Adam's children were procreations of Adam and were in "*his own likeness, and after his image*" (Genesis 5:3). Adam, like the angels had no earthly father; therefore, being direct creations of God, they were called "*sons of God*". Believers are not called "*sons of God*" until the New Testament era after the coming of the Holy Spirit in the world. John's Gospel, written to believers, says it for the first time:

"But as many as received him, to them gave he power to become the sons of God, even to them that believe on his name."
John 1:12

The Apostle Paul, agreeing with this truth, said these words:

"For as many as are led by the Spirit of God, they are the sons of God."
Romans 8:14

This means after the resurrection of Christ from the dead, He sent the Holy Ghost into the world to breathe on everyone who put their faith in the finished work of Jesus Christ. This means every believer was once dead in sins, who has been drawn by the Spirit, and delivered by the Savior are direct new creations of God the Father. Therefore, they are now called "*sons of God*". Let's read this passage in First John chapter three verse once again.

"Behold, what manner of love the Father hath bestowed upon us, that we should be called the ***sons of God****: therefore the world knoweth us not, because it knew him not."*
1 John 3:1

Never forget this fact: "***Behold***" true believers are direct New Creations of God because they are in Christ Jesus our Lord. What brought us into this new relationship with God? Three things are identified by the Apostle Paul.

*"**The grace** of the Lord Jesus Christ, and **the love** of God, and **the communion** of the Holy Ghost, be with you all. Amen."*
2 Corinthians 13:14

There it is in this one verse:

- The *grace* of the Lord Jesus - **Life**
- The ***Love*** of God
- The *communion* of the Holy Ghost - **Light**

The word "*Amen*" means "let it be so", which takes us back to the beginning when there was no rebellion, no resistance, or no retreat from God's commands. Paul is saying, agree with God: you need His grace – His love – and His communion with you. This is the promise of the *Image of God:* ***Love*** – the *Increase of Glory:* ***Life*** – and the *Influence of Goodness:* ***Light*** being restored back to true believers that was God's original design (Genesis 1:26-31).

The first description of His People is that of Love. The second description is:

Hope – Determined to be – "*like Him*" (v.2)

Faith – Declared to be – "*pure*" (v.4)

Being submerged into sonship is to have the conviction of sonship knowing the description of His people, and the conviction of sonship is having the knowledge of the:

Direction of His Purity

1 John 3:4-6

The word "*committeth*" in the Greek speaks of a consistency to sin intentionally, and the word "*transgresseth*" in the Greek speaks of consistently sinning deliberately to break God's law. John says believers are now presently the sons of God and if we have received this truth in Christ, then we prove it by keeping clean for Jesus Christ is pure and we are pure in Christ. The Apostle John reminds us:

"*And ye know that he was manifested to take away sins; and in him is no sin.*"
1 John 3:5

John says the reason why the Son of God became flesh was to destroy the works of the devil. This means there was a time when the Son of God was not flesh, but there was not a time when He was not God. Therefore, it can be said, the Son of God became the son of man so the sons of men could become sons of God. That is why the invisible God became visible (Colossians 1:13-20). The Apostle Paul said of Jesus Christ:

"*For in him dwelleth all the fulness of the Godhead bodily.*"
Colossians 2:9

Believers do sin, this is true, (1 John 1:8) but they do not go in a direction against God deliberately or intentionally consistently. The World does not know Him or His believers, but, as the sons of God, we know Him! There must be conviction of sonship. The second facet that submerges a believer into sonship is:

A Consciousness of Sonship

I John 3:7-14

It is a consciousness of extreme differences; like light and darkness noticed in Actions, Attitudes and Answers in life.

Actions

1 John 3:7,8

Note the dearness in the words "*Little children*" is an affectionate term for teachable and transforming people. They are made righteous by faith in the finished work of

Jesus Christ, who died, was buried, and rose again. They are true:

Followers of the Savior (vs.7, 9)

Therefore, they consciously think about what is right and the more they are in the Word, the Word will take root guiding every action. Righteous people want to do what is right!

The contrast, John declares, are true:

Followers of Satan (v.8)

Those who consistently commit sin are of the devil. They have no consciousness of anything different. John says the devil has been consistently doing sin from "*the beginning*" which means nothing has changed about him since he first tempted Adam and his wife causing destruction even up to this very day. He has no desire to change and those who deliberately, intentionally, and consistently follow evil will not change. There is the truth of God's Word and there is the lie of the devil; everyday there is a choice to make!

The false teaching on Sinless Perfection says we do not sin anymore after salvation, but that is a distorted view according to 1 John 3:9. John has already said in the first chapter that we deceive ourselves if we say we have no sin (1 John 1:8). John is saying that the sons of God do not walk intentionally, deliberately, and consistently into sin. John says:

"*We know that we have passed from death unto life, because we love the brethren. He that loveth not his brother abideth in death.*"
1 John 3:14

"*Death*" is existing without hope (Revelation 20:15). Do you love other believers? Do you naturally gravitate toward other believers? Do you just want to be around them; "*So much the more as you see the day approach*" (Hebrews 10:25)? True Sonship is a consciousness of extreme differences in actions. Then there is a difference in:

Attitudes

1 John 3:9-11

John, led by the Holy Spirit, uses two brothers to explain the Actions that helps us get to the root of the problem of the effects of darkness by addressing the attitudes of two brothers.

Note the hatred of Cain

Where did this hatred for his brother come from? He had offered to God an offering from his harvest as proof of his hard work from a cursed ground and the LORD had no respect for it. Cain's anger was then out of control before the LORD (Genesis 4:5). It is implied by God's statement to Cain that he knew what was expected from God.

> "*And the LORD said unto Cain, why art thou wroth? And why is thy countenance fallen? If thou doest well, shalt thou not be accepted? and if thou doest not well, sin lieth at the door. And unto thee shall be his desire, and thou shalt rule over him.*"
> Genesis 4:6, 7

God has warned Cain that his attitude left unchecked and uncorrected would result in the devil possessing him. Note the words "sin lieth at the door. And unto thee shall be his desire and thou shalt rule over him". Believers are to rule over the devil. Satan is the one not standing but lying at the door of Cain's heart. He has been cast down to the ground. He desires to rule over Cain. God says do not let him into your heart with this attitude unconverted. The contrast is in Revelation. Jesus says:

> "*Behold, I stand at the door, and knock: if any man hear my voice, and open the door, I will come in to him, and will sup with*

him, and he with me."
Revelation 3:20

Make no mistake about it, The Savior or Satan will occupy your heart. The question is, which one will you allow to rule? Cain opened his heart to Satan and under his rule Cain hates his brother and would kill.

Now, notice the contrast.

Note the love of Abel

I have said it before as a believer; I love everybody, but there are those I love, but do not like. Abel is someone I want to use to illustrate this truth. Abel loved his brother Cain, but he did not like who he had become. Therefore, out of love for him he talked to him (Genesis 4:8). The subject matter was no doubt about the issues of him being accepted by God and why.

Abel kept sheep in a vegetarian society for the purpose of clothing and cleansing that pointed to the coming of Christ: "*The Lamb of God*", of which his parents were informed of personally by God (Genesis 3:21; John 1:29).

It is hard to tell someone they are wrong, but true love delivers the mail that is consistent with God's Word. Abel was guilty, from the lost world perspective, of what would become part of the Law of the LORD, judging, and rebuking in love (Leviticus 19:15-18). Abel loved his brother but did not like what he had done.

Actions and attitudes come from the sources of a person's:

Answers

1 John 3:12-14

There are just two answers to salvation.

Cain's is Evil

Cain established a religion of salvation by works. The LORD had already established true salvation to be by grace through faith.

> "*Unto Adam also and to his wife did the LORD God make coats of skins, and clothed them.*"
> Genesis 3:21

The death of sheep done by the LORD pointed to the promise of "*The Lamb of God, which taketh away the sin of the world*" (John 1:29). Notice the singularity of the word John the Baptist used of "*sin*". John the Baptist has in mind the first sin that started all the sin in the world. There has never been another way of salvation other Jesus Christ who is the "*Alpha and the Omega, the beginning and the end*" (Revelation 1:8).

While Cain's answer to salvation is evil, John points out the fact that:

Abel's is Righteous

Salvation is by grace alone therefore Abel's sacrifice was accepted because it pointed to the love of God first manifested to his parents. Therefore, the truth is there are only really two religions in the world: One is by grace alone and the other is by works. James says our faith is seen in our works [James 2:18], but he is in harmony with the Apostle Paul that says:

> "*For by grace are you saved through faith; and that not of yourselves: it is the gift of God. Not of works, lest anyone should boast.*"
> Ephesians 2:8, 9

James is simply saying when a person has faith in the finished work of Christ, the Holy Spirit will have room to work in a person to reach out to others. Abel is accepted by what he believed, and it was evident in what he did, which is, by faith, offering up to God what the LORD had said to offer.

Abel loved Cain, but he did not like what he did, and Cain killed him for it. The same can be said of Jesus Christ who loves us but did not like what we were doing, and He was killed for it.

The World hates us, but we love them! The believer who submerges themselves into sonship has the facet of a conviction of sonship, a consciousness of sonship, and:

A Confidence Of Sonship

1 John 3:15-22

So, what is John saying we must go through to develop this confidence in the heart? He starts with:

A Compassion in the Heart

1 John 3:15-18

Those that have the life of love in them, which is the Holy Spirit, may not like others, but they love others and want others to know the truth, even if it costs them their life. Those trapped in death hate their brother, whether in actions or attitudes they are murderers, with no eternal life within. A person who has God's love within lays down their life for others. Therefore, John says:

"*Hereby perceive we the love of God, because he laid down his life for us: and we ought to lay down our lives for the brethren.*"
1 John 3:16

Believers have the bowels of compassion to give not just words of love but display actions of true love.

John says there is another thing that a true believers can know by:

A Comparison of the Heart

"And hereby we know that we are of the truth, and shall assure our hearts before him."
1 John 3:19

This is how believers know they are in Him, and He is in them. They have compassion in the heart; they have a comparison of the heart and from time to time they will have:

A Condemned Heart
1 John 3:20-22

This is not saying true believers have a condemned heart to hell, but it is saying we can be confident that the Holy Spirit gives us confidence to believe we will have a prayer answered on the behalf of others. God knows our heart and he will convict us if we do not respond to the needs of others when it is in our possession to help others. The Apostle Paul said it this way:

"But by an equality, that now at this time your abundance may be a supply for their want, that their abundance also may be a supply for your want: that there may be equality."
2 Corinthians 8:14

What is the meaning behind a believer having a condemned heart? The point John is driving home is that believers cannot just see others in need and not meet that need or at least pray that God would help that person with their need.

"And whatsoever we ask, we receive of him, because we keep his

commandments and do those things that are pleasing in his sight."
I John 3:22

The believer who submerges themselves into sonship has the facet of a conviction of sonship, a consciousness of sonship, a confidence of sonship, and:

A Commandment Of Sonship

1 John 3:22-24

Like a thread woven through the fabric of all three of John's epistles, containing only seven short chapters, is the word love, appearing thirty-four different times.[5] The Pharisees, tempting Jesus said:

"*Master, which is the great commandment in the law? Jesus said unto him, Thou shalt love the Lord thy God with all thy heart, and with all thy soul, and with all thy mind. This is the first and great commandment. And the second is like unto it, Thou shalt love thy neighbour as thyself. On these two commandments hang all the law and the prophets.*"
Matthew 22:37-40

In First John 2:8, John spoke of "*a new commandment.*" John was referring to his gospel, when he quoted our Lord on the eve of the crucifixion :

"*An new commandment I give unto you. That ye love one another; as I have loved you, that ye also love one another. By this shall all men know that ye are my disciples, if ye have love one to another.*"
John 13:34, 35

---

[5] Hawkins, O.S. THE BIBLE CODE, © 2020 by Dr. O.S. Hawkins. Published by Thomas Nelson, pp.213

True love is now expressed in the "*new commandment*".[6] The individual question is do you "*have love one another*"? This kind of "Love" supersedes and satisfies all the Ten Commandment. One word sums up all the commands according to the Apostle Paul.

"For all the law is fulfilled in one word, even in this; Thou shalt love thy neighbour as thy self."
Galatians 5:14

Conclusion

True believers have all four human facets that John has shared in this chapter, which submerges them into Sonship. They have a conviction of sonship, a consciousness of sonship, a confidence of sonship, and a commandment of sonship as they follow the Lord Jesus Christ. Our love, hope, and faith, all given to us by the Holy Spirit, sets us apart from the world (I John 3:24). Therefore, the world does not know Him or us, but as "the sons of God" we know Him (I John 3:1,2,14). The world hates us as they hated Him, but we love them as He loves them (I John 3:13,14). Led by the Holy Spirit, I think John says it best.

"Hereby perceive we the love of God, because he laid down his life for us: and we ought to lay down our lives for the brethren."
1 John 3:16

---

[6] Hawkins, O.S. THE BIBLE CODE, © 2020 by Dr. O.S. Hawkins. Published by Thomas Nelson, pp.214

CHAPTER 4
Am I Sharing the Truth in the Spirit?

1 John 4:1-21

Chapter three of First John ends with these words that lead us to the subject matter of chapter four.

"*And he that keepeth his commandments dwelleth in him, and he in him. And hereby we know that he abideth in us, by the Spirit which he hath given us.*"
1 John 3:24

The phrase "*Hereby know Ye*"," *Hereby know we*", and "*we have known*" gives us our divisions in First John chapter four. Let's get started with our fourth question:

John reminds his readers that Jesus Christ prophesied that false teachers and prophets would rise in the last days. According to the book of Hebrews chapter one the Bible says that God:

"*Hath in these last days spoken unto us by his Son, who he hath appointed heir of all things, by whom also he made the worlds.*"
Hebrews 1:2

Therefore, the term "last days" began the day Jesus started His ministry. And by the way, Jesus is still speaking through His men of God today. John says we are to "try" or test the spirits with this check list we have in this chapter because many false prophets are in the world. What are they saying? The first time we see the phrase "Hereby know ye" relates to:

The Fact of the Spirits

1 John 4:1-6a

The whole purpose of the enemy is to deceive humanity. The word for "*deceived*" is found nineteen times in the New Testament and it always has to do with the Devil and his works. The Devil does not destroy God's wheat, because he cannot do so (Luke 10:19). So, he imitates it. Wheat and tares look very much alike in the early stages of their growth, but tares are not only worthless, but they are also poisonous. God sows His children into the world, and Satan sows his counterfeit agents into the same world. Not all unbelievers are children of the Devil, the vast majority are simply unregenerated children of Adam. The "*sons of the devil*" are those people Satan has taught, inspired, energized, and sent forth as his emissaries[7].

"Beloved, believe not every spirit, but try the spirits whether they are of God: because many false prophets are gone out into the world."
1 John 4:1

There are only two types of spirits in the world. One is:

The Spirt of Christ

1 John 4:1-6a

The confession of the Spirit of God is that Jesus Christ became flesh. As I have already said, there has never been a time He was not God, but there was a time He was not flesh. It was the Spirit of God that brought to light our sin as well as our Savior. Jesus Christ, for the first time 2000 years ago, became flesh to save people who believe by faith, that Jesus

[7] Phillips, John, EXPLORING THE EPISTLES OF JOHN, © 2003 by John Phillips. Published 2003 by Kregel Publications, a division of Kregel, Inc. pp.126

came to bear their sins on the cross, died, and rose from the dead: showing that He is God.

Every spirit [person who shares their faith] that consistently confesses that Jesus Christ has come in the flesh is of God. Therefore, that is why I said, there are just two types of spirits in the world. One is the Spirit of Christ, and the other is:

The Spirit of Antichrist

1 John 4:3, 5, 6b

False prophets deny that Jesus was ever in the flesh, which is a manifest spirit of antichrist. Gnosticism is a Greek form of teaching that declared Jesus Christ was not in the flesh and their origins were in Alexandrea. They claimed to have a higher knowledge and that all flesh is sin, therefore, Jesus Christ could not be flesh.

John has shared the Fact of the Spirits; he now explains:

The Fruit of the Spirit

1 John 4:6b-10

The coming of the Holy Spirit into the world was for the express purpose of breathing His life into us that we might be "*born again*" [John 3:5-7], who were once dead in sins and trespasses (Ephesians 2:1-10). John says this about the true believers:

> "*Beloved, let us love one another: for love is of God; and every one that loveth is born of God, and knoweth God.*"
> 1 John 4:7

Only the beloved true believer can love and is commanded to consistently love because the Holy Spirit of God is within them. For a believer not to consistently love others is to grieve the Holy Spirit of God (Ephesians 4:30). So, what is the *agapan*[8] love?

Love is an expression of God (v.7)

Everyone who is "*born again*", as Jesus Christ is saying through John, consistently loves God and others. There is also the fact that:

Love is the essence of God (v.8)

John is saying, God just does not simply act in love, "*God is Love*", which is His very essence. Those who consistently love God and others really know Him. Love is the fruit of the Spirit. In Love, God has revealed to the lost world Himself in flesh as Jesus Christ for the express purpose, John says, for three reasons:

- To Reveal the Savior (v.9a)
- To Reclaim the Sinner (v.9b)
- To Reflect through the Saints (v.10)

John has shown us the Fact of the Spirits; there are many antichrist spirits in the world today, but only one Spirit of Christ. He has explained the Fruit of the Spirit which the expression of God's love and love is the essence of God. Therefore, God, who is love, dwells by faith in true believers and they reveal Him when they are:

Followers of the Spirit

1 John 4:11-16

Who can say rightly they are followers of God? Only those who are led by the Spirit can say they are true followers of God. When a person falls under the conviction of personal sin because the Holy Spirit has revealed to them the Scripture, and they by faith believe in the finished work

---

[8] Wuest, Kenneth S., "FOUR GREEK WORDS FOR LOVE", Bibliotheca Sacra (July 1959). pp.27

of the Savior, then are they ready to respond to His salvation. They Admit they are a sinner; they Believe on the Son of God [*His death, burial, and resurrection*], and Confess Him as their Lord. That is the ABC's of the Gospel. The Apostle Paul said:

"*For as many as are led by the Spirit of God, they are the sons of God*"
Romans 8:14

For those who are in doubt of their personal salvation, John says three things stand out with true followers of the Spirit.

They Perform in the Love of God

"*Beloved, if God so love us, we ought to love one another.*"
1 John 4:11

They are Perfected in the Love of God

"*No man hath seen God at any time. If we love one another, God dwelleth in us, and his love is perfected in us.*"
1 John 4:12

They are Presently in the Love of God

"*Hereby know we that we dwell in him, and he in us, because he hath given us of his Spirit. And we have seen and do testify that the Father sent the Son to be the Saviour of the world. Whosoever shall confess that Jesus is the Son of God, God dwelleth in him, and he in God. And we have known and believed the love that God hath to us. God is love; and he that dwelleth in love dwelleth in God, and God in him.*"

1 John 4:13-16

With confidence, John says, regarding true followers of God, "*we have known and believe the love of God*" (1 John 4:16a). What is it we know?

We now have the Spirit of God (v.13,14)

"*God is Light*"

"*Hereby know*" – You know because

"*The Spirit itself beareth witness with our spirit, that we are the children of God.*"
Romans 8:16

"*For ye are all the children of God by faith in Christ Jesus*"
Galatians 3:26

We are His offspring, for "*according to his abundant mercy [he] hath begotten us again*" (1 Peter 1:3). As His children, we ever look like Him, in a spiritual sense, "*partakers of the divine nature*" [2 Peter 1:4], and His Fatherly love surrounds us.

We now are in the Son of God (v.15)

"*God the Life*"

"*Jesus is the son of God.*" John keeps stressing this great truth. "*God sent his Son into the world, that we might live through him*" (1 John 4:9). "*The Father sent the Son to be the Savior of the world*" (1 John 4:14). "*[He] sent his Son to be the propitiation for our sins*" (1 John 4:9, 10, 14). "*He that hath the Son hath life*" (1 John 5:12). And "*Whosever shall confess that Jesus is the Son of God, God dwelleth in him, and he in God*" (1 John 4:14). We must confess, unequivocally and without reservation, that Jesus is the Son of God.

Yet one influential pastor-teacher takes the position that "*Eternally He is God, but only from His incarnation has He been the Son: Christ was not Son until His incarnation.*" The teaching, known as "*incarnational Sonship*," has been around for a long time, and it sounds plausible. The only problem is that it is simply not true[9].

We now are in God the Father (v.16)

"*God is Love*"

It must ring through our belief: "*And we have known and believed the love that God hath to us*" [4:16]; and it must resound in our behavior: "*God is love; and he that dwelleth in God, and God in him*" (1 John 4:16b). God loves us. God is love. We love. God dwells in us. John never gets tired of ringing the changes on this great theme[10].

The Apostle Paul says:

"*And if children, then heirs; heirs of God and joint-heirs with Christ; if so be that we suffer with him, that we may be also glorified together.*"
Romans 8:17

The question was asked one time to Jesus Christ by one shaken disciple:

"*How is it that thou wilt manifest thyself unto us, and not unto the world? Jesus answered and said unto him, If a man love me, he will keep my words: and my Father will love him, and we will come unto him, and make our abode with him. He that loveth me not keepeth not my sayings: and the word which ye hear is not mine, but the Father's which sent me. These things have I spoken unto you, being yet present with you. But the Comforter, which is the Holy Ghost,*

---

[9] Phillips, John, EXPLORING THE EPISTLES OF JOHN, © 2003 by John Phillips. Published 2003 by Kregel Publications, a division of Kregel, Inc. pp.146

[10] - - - pp.147

whom the Father will send in my name, he shall teach you all things, and bring all things to your remembrance, whatsoever I have said unto you."
John 14:22-26

True believers can say with conviction that where the fruit of the Spirit is there is comfort, which is the sign of the Spirit and where we have followers of the Spirit, we have the Love of God revealed. Our purpose is to glorify our Creator as Love, Life, and Light to others.

John has uncovered the Facts of the Spirits, the Fruit of the Spirit, Following the Spirit, and now he covers the:

Formation of the Spirit

1 John 4:17-21

A follower in the Spirit is not perfect, but the Spirit in them leads them with Scripture developing their faith, Sharing their faith, and with daily Situations of Faith.

Scripture develops our Faith

Scripture understood by the Spirit is Light to a believer.

"Herein is our love made perfect, that we may have boldness in the day of judgement: because as he is so, are we in the world." I John 4:17

Sharing our Faith

Sharing our faith is the Love of God the Father expressed to others.

"*There is no fear in love; but perfect love casteth out fear: because fear hath torment, He that feareth is not made perfect in love. We love*

him, because he first loved us."
1 John 4:18,19

Situations of Faith

Situations of Faith reveals the Life of Christ in us.

"*If a man say, I love God, and hateth his brother, he is a liar: for he that loveth not his brother whom he hath seen, how can he love God whom he hath not seen? And this commandment have we from him, That he who loveth God love his brother also.*"
1 John 4:20, 21

Growing up in the faith is scary sometimes. We face a lot of choices to make that have consequences and as well obstacles of the devil. John has not been talking about a spirit of bondage, but the freedom of believers. The Apostle Paul reminds us:

"*For ye have not received the spirit of bondage again to fear; but ye have received the Spirit of adoption, whereby we cry, Abba, Father*"
Romans 8:15

God's people stand out in a world of spirits as Love, in true Life, and as the Light of heaven in the darkness of night. King Solomon says it this way:

"*But the path of the just is as the shining light, that shineth more and more unto the perfect day.*"
Proverbs 4:18

That Great Morning is coming when the Son of God will catch-up the saints that where He is we will be also (John 14:3). That is our blessed hope. Then we will take part behind our King of kings and LORD of lords in His glorious appearing (John 14:3; Titus 2:13; Revelation 19:11-16).

Conclusion

All true believers are indwelled with the Spirit of God (Romans 8:9). True Spirit-filled people will consistently confess that Christ has come in the flesh. John is one of our examples of how sharing Christ proves we are filled with the Spirit (1 John 4:13-16). There can be no excuse acceptable by God for holding on to the fear of testifying of Christ to your fellowman, for love moves us to share.

"Perfect love casteth out fear"
1 John 4:18

CHAPTER 5
Am I Saved for Sure?
1 John 5:1-21

Regarding salvation, "*know*" is a big subject in this chapter. The phrases "*we know*", "*Ye may know*", and "*we may know*" are a total of eight times in First John, chapter five. Eight is the Hebrew numerical number for "*new beginnings*". The central focus of this chapter is that you may know.

"*He that hath the Son hath life; and he that hath not the Son of God hath not life. These things have I written unto you that believe on the name of the Son of God; that ye may know that ye have eternal life, and that ye may believe on the name of the Son of God.*"
1 John 5:12, 13

Our first subject in this chapter is:

Saving Faith
1 John 5:1-5

Truly saved people are born of God by the Scripture, the Spirit, and the Savior (John 3:3-16). The Apostle Paul said:

"*For ye are all the children of God by faith in Christ Jesus.*"
Galatians 3:26

The Apostle Peter, declaring true believers to be God's offspring, said:

"*According to his abundant mercy [he] hath begotten us again*"
1 Peter 1:3

Luke, the writer of the book of Acts, quoting the Apostle Paul, wrote:

"For in him we live, and move, and have our being; as certain also of your own poets have said, For we are also his offspring, Forasmuch then as we are the offspring of God, we ought not to think that the Godhead is like unto gold, or silver, or stone, graven by art and man's device. And the times of this ignorance God winked at; but now commandeth all men every where to repent. Because he hath appointed a day, in the which he will judge the world in righteousness by that man whom he hath ordained; whereof he hath given assurance unto all men, in that he hath raise him from the dead."
Acts 17:29-31

We have already covered the matter of off-spring in chapter three. Therefore, staying with the subject, Saving Faith:

Is Ongoing Faith
1 John 5:1-3

Notice three consistencies within ongoing faith. Ongoing Faith:

Has consistent Life in His Son (v.1)
"*believeth*"

The word "*believeth*" in the Greek means a consistent ongoing matter, which in context is real faith. Jesus is the anointed one, which is the meaning of the word "*Christ*"[11]. There is only one anointed. Believers in Him have acknowledged they are anointed from above by Him, who is with them, and in them (Ephesians 4:6).
Ongoing Faith also:

---

[11] 3,458 BIBLE PEOPLE & PLACES, Copyright © 1993 by Thomas Nelson, Inc. First Inspirational Press edition published in 2001. pp.189

Has consistent Light in His Spirit (v.2)

"we know"

John says "*we know*" we are believers when we love God and others as spelled out in all the commandments. Once again, never forget, Jesus said "*On these two commandments hang all the law and the prophets*" (Matthew 22:40). The phrase "*all the law and the prophets*" is reference to all the Old Testament. Ongoing faith is consistent life, consistent light, and thirdly, it:

Has consistent Love in God the Father (v.3)

"this is the love of God"

A believer has evidence in them when, out of His love, we want to consistently keep His commandments. We do not keep His commandment to be saved. We keep His commandments because we are saved. We love Him and by the Holy Spirit in us we want to keep his commandments. John says: "*His commandments are not grievous.*" John is the one who recorded Jesus' one commandment that simplified all the commandments: "*That ye love one another; as I have loved you, that ye also love one another*" (John 13:34). The Apostle Paul simplifies it to just one word.

"For all the law is fulfilled in one word, even in this; Thou shalt love thy neighbor as thyself."
Galatians 5:14

True faith consistently loves Him [God] and them [those around us]. "*We know*" loving them is loving Him as commanded by God (1 John 5:2,3). Consistent love is the commandments kept.

Saving Faith is ongoing faith. Also Saving faith:

Is Overcoming Faith

1 John 5:4,5

In this world, a lot of stuff is thrown at Christians. True born-again believers overcome the world, which is the victory of real faith. Those with victorious faith believe in who Jesus is! We are to have peace in this troubled world. For as Jesus Christ has overcome the world, so have we that are in HIM (John 16:33)!

We have just covered five verses on the grace of Saving Faith. Now let us look at some:

Sovereign Facts

1 John 5:6-12

What John is informing us of is not his opinion, but the message from our Sovereign God. The first of these facts is the clarity of:

The Truth of God

1 John 5:6

John has already recorded this message for us in the gospel of John and we must keep these words of Jesus Christ in our minds as we interpret this text. Jesus clearly told His followers:

"*I am the way, the truth, and the life: no man cometh unto the Father, but by me.*"
John 14:6

The article "*the*" used three times here expresses the narrow way to heaven, which is Jesus Christ alone. Jesus did not say I am "a" way which would have implied more than one way to heaven. "*The way*" is narrow, absolute, and emphatic.

Jesus Christ is declaring without a doubt that all other ways to heaven are false and frauds.

Jesus came to fulfill the scripture, which is the "*water*" that helps believers keep clean (Ephesians 5:26). Jesus came to satisfy God's righteous demands, promised from the foundation of the world by the sacrifice of a lamb [Genesis 3:15, 21], which was the Alpha sacrifice of the promise of His "*blood*". Jesus came to bear witness of "*the Spirit of Truth*" which is the fact that God loves us; overturning the lie implied by the serpent (Genesis 3:4,5).

The second Sovereign Fact is the clarity of:

The Tri-unity of God

1 John 5:7

John says the Tri-unity of God, is the record in heaven now revealed to true believers.

- ➢ God the Father
- ➢ God the Son
- ➢ God the Holy Ghost

"*These three are one*" (1 John 5:7). John says the Tri-unity of God, which is one, is the record in heaven and only true believers will bear witness of this fact.

The third Sovereign Fact clarified is:

The Testimony of God

1 John 5:8

The testimony of God or "*the three that bear witness*" John says by the Holy Spirit is now in the earth. They are as follows.

- ➢ The Spirit
- ➢ The Scripture – "*the water*"

As we have already shown, water in type is a reference to

the Scripture. The Scripture is revealed to us by the Holy Spirit. The gospel of John says, referring to Jesus Christ, "*the Word was made flesh and dwelled among us, (and we beheld his glory, the glory as of the only begotten of the Father,) full of grace and truth*" (John 1:14).

The third thing that bears witness in the earth is:

- The Sacrifice – "*the blood*"

John says: "*these three agree in one*", which implies to the oneness in Christ we have in the earth. It is all Christ!

The Teachers of God

1 John 5:9-12

John says:

> "*If we receive the witness of men, the witness of God is greater: for this is the witness of God which he hath testified of his Son. He that believeth on the Son of God hath the witness in himself: he that believeth not God hath made him a liar; because he believeth not the record that God gave of his Son. He that hath the Son hath life; and he that hath not the Son of God hath not life.*"
>
> 1 John 5:9-12

So, what are the facts that reveal the teachers of God? True teachers of God:

- **Teach the Word of God** (v.9)

The witness of God is greater than the witness of men. What was the testimony of the Son of God – "*God so loved the world, that he gave his only begotten son*" (John 3:16a). The word "*begotten*" means the only promised son! For instance, Abraham had two sons Ishmael and Isaac, but only Isaac was the promised son (Hebrew 11:17).

- **Believe the Record of God** (v.10)

Those who consistently believe Jesus is the Son of God who died and rose again has the Holy Spirit in them. They believe God's record "*that whosoever believeth in him should not perish*" (John 3:16b). To not believe the record of God is to make Him out to be a liar and are identified as illegitimate and they will pass away (1 John 5:10).

o **Have eternal Life in God** (vs.11,12)
Those who have eternal life in God are in Christ. Once again, "*this is the record, that God hath given to us eternal life, and this life is in his Son*" (1 John 5:11). Jesus declared that God's love received by the believer is "*everlasting life*" (John 3:16). That is what He said! He also said:

"My sheep hear my voice, and I know them, and they follow me: And I give unto them eternal life; and they shall never perish, neither shall any man pluck them out of my hand. My Father, which gave them me, is greater than all; and no man is able to pluck them out of my Father's hand. I and my Father are one."
John 10:27-30

The Apostle Paul explains that true believers are "*sealed with that holy Spirit of promise, which is the earnest of our inheritance until the redemption of the purchased possession, unto the praise of his glory*" (Ephesians 1:13,14). True teachers of God teach the Word of God, believe the Record of God, and have eternal Life in God.

We have just covered seven verses that gives us the perfection of Sovereign Facts. Now that we are near the finish of this first epistle of John, we are given John's central theme of the book. We can know we are:

Saved Forever
1 John 5:13-21

Nine verses reveal the believer who is Saved Forever. The word "*know*" is found seven times in these last nine verses. John wants his readers to "*know*" for sure they are saved forever. Within these last nine verses contain four elements that can help a follower to know they are Saved Forever. First there is:

Clarity of Life

"*He that hath the Son hath life; and he that hath not the Son of God hath not life.*"
1 John 5:12

Have the Son, have Life – Have not the Son, have not Life.

The word "*life*" is the Greek word *zoe*. To have HIM, that is Jesus Christ the Son of God, is to have eternal life. *zoe* is not a temporal life by any means. Jesus did not say He had life. He is the essence of Life. All true life is of Him, in Him, for Him, and held together by HIM; He has the preeminence (Colossians 1:16-19). This word "*preeminence*" means first place. Does Jesus Christ have first place in your life? If so, John says there will be:

Confirmation of Life

"*These things have I written unto you that believe on the name of the Son of God; that ye may know that ye have eternal life, and that ye may believe on the name of the Son of God.*"
1 John 5:13

John is saying to his readers, who are seekers of Christ, that he has written under the power of the Holy Spirit this epistle for the express purpose that "*ye may know*" if you are saved or not. It is through prayer and persistency that proof of spirit can be confirmed. The spirit in a person is the part of a person that studies and thinks. For example: Jesus said to His learners:

"These things have I spoken unto you, being yet present with you. But the Comforter, which is the Holy Ghost, whom the Father will send in my name, he shall teach you all things, and bring back all things to your remembrance, whatsoever I have said unto you."
John 14:25, 26

Are you a thinking, teachable, and trainable truth seeker? If so, let me remind you once again. The Bible says:

"The Spirit itself beareth witness with our spirit, that we are the children of God."
Romans 8:16

It takes the Scripture and the Spirit to reflect the Savior in a person. That is the clarity that leads to conformation. Then comes the:

Confidence of Life

1 John 5:14-20

When a person's pattern for life is the Scriptures and their prayer life is in the Spirit, John declares:

"And this is the confidence that we have in him, that, if we ask any thing according to his will, he heareth us; And if we know that he hear us, whatsoever we ask, we know we have the petitions that we desired of him."
1 John 5:14,15

Note the words "*according to his will*", which is very important, for it implies that we are to have an understanding from Scripture of the will of God in advance to the prayer request made in His name that precedes an answered prayer. John then points out how punishment in life can negatively affect the confidence in a person's prayer life for someone.

> "*If any man see his brother sin a sin which is not unto death, he shall ask, and he shall give him life for them that sin not unto death. There is a sin unto death: I do not say that he shall pray for it. All unrighteousness is sin: and there is a sin not unto death.*"
> 1 John 5:16,17

You might say: What is "*a sin unto death*"? Is all sin the same? Do we have any examples in Scripture? Here are three examples from Scripture for your consideration. Moses committed a sin unto death [Numbers 20:12], the Prophet Hananiah [Jeremiah 28:1-17], and in the New Testament there is Ananias and his wife Sapphira (Acts 5:1-11).

I will expound on Moses and leave the other two examples for you to study for yourselves. Moses struck the rock because God commanded so in Numbers 17:6. According to the Apostle Paul, this was a picture or type of Christ God in the Old Testament (1 Corinthians 10:4). The type was clear that Christ died once for all the world. Now back to Moses. The second time the people needed water God said for Moses to speak to the Rock [Jesus would only die once not twice] and rebelliously before the people Moses struck the rock (Numbers 20:7-13). Moses in anger disobeyed God and God would not allow him to go into the promised land. Moses would keep on praying for God to allow him to go over, but God finally forbid Moses from even praying for such a request (Deuteronomy 3;25,26). Yes, Moses lived to be One hundred- and twenty-years-old, but note what was said of him the day of his death:

> "*And Moses was an hundred and twenty years old when he died: his eyes were not dim, nor his natural forces abated.*"
> Deuteronomy 34:7

This verse is telling us that Moses could have lived a lot longer. The devourer was rebuked by God over Moses during his life (Malachi 3:11). His clothing did not wear out (Deuteronomy 8:4). His shoes did not wear out (Deuteronomy 29:5). His feet did not swell (Nehemiah 9:21). Sin always has consequences. Moses is a prime example of a person who commits a "*sin unto death*" (1 John 5:16). The thing we must never forget is the fact that Moses never lost his eternal relationship with God. Even at his death we are told that the angel Michael rebuked the Devil in the name of the LORD over the body of Moses (Jude 9). Therefore, John is saying believers can have confidences in life that they are saved by their prayers being answered that are prayed within the will of God, and they cannot expect a favorable answer when they pray for a person who has committed a sin unto death.

John moves on to another phrase that confirms life when he says:

*"**We know** that whosever is born of God sinneth not: but he that is begotten of God keepeth himself, and that wicked one touched him not. And **we know** that we are of God, and the whole world lieth in wickedness."*

1 John 5:18,19

Here, John is just restating the truth he has already covered in chapter 3:3-6, that a true believer cannot consistently, repetitiously, and intentionally commit sin. They have the Holy Spirit in them that will convict their conscience until they come clean. Like Moses in Jude 9, "the wicked one toucheth him not" (I John 5:18). The true believer knows that the whole world lieth in wickedness, which means believers can fall in this world, but we keep standing up by the grace of God (I John 5:19). By the Spirit in us, we know we are saved!

Confidence of Life is known by the truly saved because in the Spirit we also know our Savior.

"And we know that the Son of God is come, and hath given us an

understanding, that we may know him that is true, and we are in him that is true, even in his Son Jesus Christ. This is the true God, and eternal life."
1 John 5:20

Just note what John says about those who have eternal life and what they "*know*" about Christ. We know He is coming. We know in Him we are compete. We know He is the Christ. Note the three different phrases in these last eight verses that include the word "*know*". Just look at what John is saying when these phrases are placed alongside each other:
"*Ye may know*" what "*we know*" that it is a fact "*that we may know Him*".

Now, who is Jesus Christ?
"*This is the true God, and eternal life.*"
John is just restating what all the Apostles knew and we should know. Jesus Christ is the image of the invisible God (Colossians 1:15). In Jesus Christ consistently dwells all the fullness of the Godhead bodily, and we are complete in HIM (Colossians 2:9,10). Our life is hidden with Christ in God (Colossians 3:3).
John has shown us that believers can know they are Saved Forever through clarity of life, confirmation of life, and confidence in life that now fits perfectly with this final:

Command of Life

"*Little children, keep yourselves from idols. Amen.*"
1 John 5:21

Living out his final days in Ephesus, the great centers of idolatry in the Roman world, John saw as we are now seeing in our day ample possibilities to compromise. Anything you put your trust in whether personal works, wealth, or worldly wisdom can become an idol.

Conclusion

As faithful servants and stewards of God, may we raise the children born to us or simply around us in *the fear of God, the fire of the Holy Spirit, and the faith of a little child that was exemplified perfectly for us in the Son of God.* We are redeemed by Him, rejected in the earth, received in glory, and always to be a reflection of Him while we are here. The Believer's life is to be lived as an exclamation mark, not a question mark! The last word is "*Amen*" [meaning *let it be so*]. Is your life an echo of this truth: "*Let it be so*" in me?

SUMMERY

If you are still not yet sure you are saved, just look at what John's motivation and message is to his students of the Word; just consider for a moment how each chapter starts.

Chapter one – **Foundational** - "*That which was from the beginning… the Word of God*" (1 John 1:1).

Chapter two – **Faith** - "*My little children*" (1 John 2:1). This term "*little children*" is a holy, humble, and honorable position. Jesus Christ, defining the greatest in heaven, called a little child unto Himself and said to His followers:

"*Whosoever therefore shall humble himself as this little child, the same is greatest in the kingdom of Heaven.*"
Matthew 18:4

Chapter three – **Family** – "*Behold, what manner of love…we…the sons of God*" (1 John 3:1).

Chapter four – **Fullness** - "*Beloved, believe not every spirit…Jesus Christ is come in the flesh…to be the propitiation for our sins…God is love*" (1 John 4:1,2,10,16).

Chapter five – **Forever** – "*Whosoever believeth that Jesus is the Christ is born of God…ye have eternal life*" (1 John 5:1,13).

"*The **grace of the Lord Jesus Christ**, and the **love of God**, and the **communion of the Holy Ghost**, be with you all. Amen.*"
2 Corinthians 13:14

ABOUT THE AUTHOR

Since 1994, Dr. Jeff I. Parker has pastored three churches in the Carolinas. "A Church of Meaningful Relationships" has been his vision for ministry. A Relationship Ultimately with God, United as Family, and Uniquely with Others to reach the world with the message of the Gospel of the Lord Jesus Christ.
A graduate of Fruitland Baptist Bible College. He holds an earned Th.D. from Andersonville Baptist Theological Seminary. His first book was published in 2008; Biblical Answers to Doctrinal Questions.
Jeff and his wife Priscilla have three children and guardianship of Alexia Church. They have ten grandchildren.

www.ingramcontent.com/pod-product-compliance
Lightning Source LLC
LaVergne TN
LVHW091224150826
845673LV00003B/1001